Changing Your Life Through Mindfulness:

How To Live The Successful Happy Life You Desire

Jennifer N. Smith

Introduction

What would you do if you knew you could change your life forever, simply by becoming more mindful? That by doing so, you could not only improve your happiness, but become more successful and even improve your health?

Most of us live our lives on autopilot. We get out of bed, make coffee, shower, brush our teeth, and maybe have a bit to eat and we are out the door. Perhaps there have been times when you arrive at work without any recollection of how you even got there. Most of us spend our day doing our jobs as if we are some kind of robot, then drive home and start our evening routine.

Days, weeks and months pass by without us even realizing it; then suddenly, we feel as if we have just woken up, as if we had been living in a haze all our live. That's when most of us know that something needs to change.

What has happened is that everything in your life has become a habit. No longer do we focus on what we are doing, but instead we allow our bodies to take over while our minds are elsewhere. "What do I have to do when I get home? What am I going to have for dinner? Did I turn off the coffee pot? Will the babysitter be at the bus stop in time to pick up my kids?" – We are constantly in a state of worrying, overthinking, planning and remembering.

As a matter of fact: we have stopped living in the present and instead, we allow our minds to worry about the future and even the past events, when what really matters is the present.

What have you been thinking about while you have been reading the past few paragraphs? Have you really been focused on the words that you have been reading or have you been focused on other things that are going on in your life?

I challenge you this: as you read through the rest of this book, you begin being mindful of what you are doing instead of thinking about everything else that is going on around you and in your life. **That is your first step to changing your life, becoming a happier person than you are now - a more successful and a healthier person.**

However, there is much more to mindfulness than to simply pay attention to what you are doing right now, and your present. If there was not, we could end this book right here and call it a day; but what you are going to learn throughout the rest of this book is how mindfulness affects every area of your life, and how it can make your life better.

Chapter 1- What Is Mindfulness?

As you have already learned in the introduction of this book, mindfulness involves focusing on what you are doing right now, but you have also learned that it is much more than that. In order for you to truly understand what mindfulness is, you have to put it into practice in your life. This is what I intend to focus on in this chapter.

In short, mindfulness means that we become aware of what is going on right now, and that we do not focus on anything else but the way our body feels at this moment, what we are doing, how we are feeling, what our thoughts are and on our environment.

Important: while we are focusing on all of these things, it is important that we are not judgmental of them but that we accept them without judgment. Many of us have been taught that there is a right and a wrong way for us to feel at any given moment. We think we are supposed to be perky and happy when we wake up but when we feel exhausted, we begin judging ourselves because of the way we feel. We start the morning by telling ourselves that we are being lazy, and that we should not feel tired or that it is wrong for us to feel tired.

This is just one example, but I am sure that you can think of a million times in your life where you have been judgmental toward yourself simply because of the way you were feeling.

Mindfulness is also about leaving the past in the past. This means that instead of wasting your time rehashing events that have happened in the past, letting them take control over your mind and your feelings, you finally become aware of how you feel NOW. You do not focus on the things of the past because you finally understand that everything that has happened to you was in the past and there is nothing you can do about it now.

This also allows you to stop worrying about the future. We all do it, some of us more than others. Worrying is a natural part of our life, and there isn't much we can do to stop ourselves from overthinking about the future. We plan for the future meticulously and something completely different happens in real life, so that's all our time wasted. So,
really what does this worry do for you?

The truth is that overthinking and worrying about the future doesn't really help us in any way. But, focusing on right now, focusing on the things that you can do right now and focusing on the moment that you are living, ensures that you can have the future that you've always wanted. Living in the moment means that you take away the worry and allow yourself to accept whatever happens, just because you know it is going to be positive.

People who practice mindfulness, do not allow their lives to pass them by while they worry about the past or imagine what the future will be like; but instead, they take part in every moment of their lives making it what they want it to be.

A part of mindfulness is connected to meditation, and this comes from the root of mindfulness. Mindfulness is practiced by the Buddhists, but has become more mainstream and less religious in recent days. Many people have also become aware of the benefits of meditation and because of this, they have incorporated this technique in their life as well. However, it is completely understandable if you are afraid meditation might interfere with your religious beliefs. Although, there is no way for me to convince you otherwise, personally, I feel that it is important for everyone to understand that meditation is nothing religious. Meditation is a practice, not a belief.

Mindfulness meditation is simply the act of focusing on what you are doing in the present moment. You can use deep breathing exercises, guided meditations or any other process that you want, **but you will get the same result and that is a happier, more successful, healthier you.**

Mindfulness is a technique that will turn off the autopilot that handles your present life and will help you get into manual mode - for lack of better words. It will make you become aware of what you are doing, instead of living your life feeling as if you are in some dream state. It allows you to pay attention to life, to let you feel however you want to feel without facing judgment; it is going to create a space in this world for you to live, feel and think however you want to without worrying about being in the wrong.

Some of the greatest people in history have been the ones that do not think or feel the way other people have told them to. Even people that you do not know personally but only by reputation, i.e. the people you know of who are successful and live a life that is, by your standard, what you want – can influence you in your decisions. Let me tell you why they are the ones with a different life and lifestyle!

Unlike most of the population who abide by the standard thought pattern of society, they prefer to think, feel and do what they think is right.

I am not saying they all practice the art of mindfulness in order to do so, but they do live their life exactly as they want to. Instead of spending too much time in the past or the future, they live in the present. Why am I focusing on this? Because it allows you to know that you do not have to conform to what society thinks you should become but that you can and will watch your dreams come true.

Mindfulness is based on being conscious of every moment in your life, however, it also has to do with not forgetting and reducing the confusion in your life.

We have all at some point in our lives forgotten something crucial, because our minds were elsewhere; we have all found ourselves confused at some point of our lives because we were unsure what was really going on. However, when you practice mindfulness, all of this goes away. Instead of focusing on what you are going to make for dinner while someone is speaking to you, you are going to focus on exactly what is being said. This will allow you to recall it later and when you need that information; you won't find yourself staring blankly into someone's face as you try to remember what was said at your earlier meeting, because all you can remember is the pasta recipe you wanted to make for dinner. You would have completely missed out on important information and news because you were so unnecessarily engrossed in thinking about dinner.

While mindfulness was used in religious practices of the past, it has become extremely popular in today's society as people are becoming aware of the need for it. Many of us growing up dreamed of living a fast-paced life; I know I did. Growing up in a sleepy small town, my dreams were always big, and filled with being a busy, important adult with thousands of chores and duties on my head. However, what I, like many other people, have found out is that it is not as fun as we once thought it would be. Actually, it is very stressful life to live, and that maybe, that slow paced sleepy lifestyle wasn't so bad after all!

The problem is that: there is no going back. You can't go back and tell that little kid that their dreams are wrong, and even if you could, it would not do much good.

This is just what society is today. We all live a fast-paced life. We all find ourselves multitasking just to get everything done, sleeping less than we know we should because there is so much to get done. Still, we are not able to accomplish it all, because there isn't enough time to do everything we want to do.

With all of these responsibilities, there is no time to worry about the things that have happened in the past. With so much to accomplish, we simply don't have enough time to waste replaying events that have happened to us in the past. At the same time, while we would love to spend our days dreaming of some amazing future, there is also no time for that. And don't think we don't know it, because we do. **Knowing we can't spare our precious, limited time, we still find ourselves taking part in it.**

That is where mindfulness comes in.

Now I want to make it very clear that mindfulness is not just becoming aware of what you are doing. There is a huge difference in awareness and mindfulness. Awareness is simply one of the steps that you will have to take in order to reach mindfulness. There is no way that you can attain mindfulness simply by becoming aware. There is much, much more into it.

Mindfulness is a way for you to get around the daily stresses that you will face in your life. It is great for those who are feeling so overwhelmed with their lives that they are not really living at all.

Mindfulness is about being mentally present where you physically are.

Did that make sense? Let me explain.

It is about waking up and taking a few minutes to experience waking up; what is doesn't mean is that you jump out of your bed, already worrying about your first meeting of the day. It is about experiencing the act of walking while you are walking, experiencing your shower, your food, and even your breaths. What it doesn't mean is to automatically go through your daily rituals without even being aware of what you are doing, having your breakfast in a hurry and instantly forgetting what your food tasted like.

When you practice mindfulness, every area of your life really does change. Instead of eating in front of the television, you will learn to practice mindfulness while you are eating, which means that while you are eating, you will simply just eat, being aware of every single mouthful, and being aware of how your food tastes. This will provide you with a lot of other benefits, something which we will discuss later in this book.

Chapter 2- Benefits of Practicing Mindfulness

With all of the technology that we are exposed to every single day, it is no wonder how many of us actually feel as if we can go through our days without using them. Our brains have literally become addicted to the stimulation that is provided by all of the technology that are so readily available to us, and the stress that we deal with each day.

In order to break this addiction, you have to practice mindfulness.

However, mindfulness should never become just one more thing that you have to get done in your day. You need to immediately stop practicing mindfulness the moment it becomes something "to get through" every day, or something on your to-do list. Why? Because, you see, mindfulness is not just something that you do, **it is a state of being,** it should be who you are. If it feels like a task, a chore that has to be completed, then you are not doing it right. You'll only be adding something to your list that you think you should be doing, not enjoying it or getting any benefits from it.

Many people ask themselves if they should take part in mindfulness, they wonder if it is going to benefit them. Trust me when I tell you this: no matter who you are or what you do in your life, mindfulness is going to benefit you. Personally, I also think that it is important for you to understand all of the benefits of mindfulness if you are seriously thinking of trying it out.

Mindfulness helps to reduce stress in a person's life. **Studies have shown that while mindfulness is not going to reduce the <u>stressors</u> in a person's life, it does help increase happiness and it affects the way that a person reacts to their personal stressors.**

We all know how stress can affect our health. It can cause us to gain weight, increase our chances of heart disease, causes high blood pressure and so much more, but this only happens if we do not know how to deal with the stress. When you practice mindfulness, you no longer allow stress to affect you. Instead, you simply deal with the problem and move on to the next moment in your life.

The second and possibly, one of the most important, benefit of practicing mindfulness is that it allows us to get to know our true selves. You may be sitting there telling yourself that you do know who you are and that no one knows you better than you do, but I can vehemently challenge that. No matter who we are, we tend to look at our lives and ourselves with rose-colored glasses. We tend to think that we work harder than those around us, that what we are doing is more important than what other people are doing, and that we are simply better all-around than other people are.

While there may be many things in your life that you are really good at, it is important for you to learn how to be honest with yourself, and that is what mindfulness is going to teach you to do. No, it is not about pointing out your flaws and feeling poorly about yourself, but instead, it is about identifying the areas of your life which can be improved, doing so without feeling judged and being able to improve them. Mindfulness is going to take your attention off those that are around you and it is going to bring your attention back to you, where it belongs. You can finally focus on what's most important: you, your life, your surroundings.

Not only does mindfulness allow you to get to know who you really are but it is going to help you get to know who the people around you truly are. It will allow you to take away the projections that you put onto other people and really get to know who they are, not who you want them to be.

One of the great benefits of mindfulness is that it makes everything in life so much better. Have you ever wakened up in the morning and looked around your room suddenly realizing how great your life is?

Have you ever really realized just how lucky you are to have the job that you have or how much you really love the little things in life? Times like this are fleeting.

Mindfulness can help you produce a higher quality of work. When you begin to practice mindfulness, you will find that you are better able to focus on the work that you are doing.

Whether is school work or your job, you will be able to truly focus on what's important at the moment. You will become more productive as well, because instead of focusing on everything, you will be able to focus on what you are doing.

It can help you to reduce the pain that you deal with every day. If you suffer from chronic pain, have back aches, bad migraines or cramps, or if you just have to deal with pain, you know how distracting it can be. From the pain that is caused from arthritis to the pain that is caused from a toothache, mindfulness helps to reduce it all. When mindfulness first made its way to the US, it was used as a way to reduce pain for people that mainstream medicine was unable to help. By practicing mindfulness, people were able to live a more normal life, one that was filled with pleasure instead of always focusing on the pain that they were feeling.

Mindfulness is also a great way to protect the mind and help reduce the chances of developing a mental illness. It can really help people who already suffer from a mental illness, by reducing the severity of their symptoms.

Many mental illnesses are caused by fear and stress. By becoming mindful and practicing mindfulness, you can learn to handle these fears, these stresses and soon you will find that you do not suffer from the mental disorders that once plagued you.

One of the greatest benefits of mindfulness is that it makes everything in life so much better. Have you ever wakened up in the morning and looked around your room suddenly realizing how great your life is?

Have you ever really realized just how lucky you are to have the job that you have or how much you really love the little things in life? Times like this are fleeting, and still we don't pay much attention to them. With mindfulness, you'll be able to live each of these precious moments as they come to you, instead of just letting them pass.

When you practice mindfulness and you, for example, take a shower, you become mindful of everything within that shower. You really experience the water, you experience the feel of the washcloth on your skin and the smell of the shampoo in your hair. You finally get to feel the relaxed enjoyment of simply being in the shower instead of rushing through the process because the only thing that you can think about is the next thing on your to-do list that you have to get done.

Using mindfulness is going to allow you to <u>enjoy</u> every single activity that you take part in every day, from exercising to eating your simple meals, to lying down on your comfortable bed and falling asleep at night.

It allows you to really experience life instead of just trudging through it. It can even make the music that you listen to sound better because it will allow you to become more aware of each note that is played and every word that is spoken.

You may have simply hummed along your favorite tunes in the past, but with mindfulness, you can actually pay attention to the depth of the words used.

Mindfulness helps us even when we are not purposefully practicing it. When you begin, you will learn to start off using mindful meditation. When you practice meditation, you are literally changing the way that your brain works. **Practicing meditation is almost the same as rewiring your brain.** You get to choose how your brain reacts, thinks and works. This means that even when you are not meditating, you will find yourself naturally more aware of everything that's going on around you, what you are thinking and what you are feeling. Mindfulness will actually become something that you do not have to think about, but instead comes completely naturally.

When you use mindfulness, you will find that you have suddenly become more self-aware, but that you become more sympathetic to those that come to you for help. If you are like me, your friends and family often come to you for your advice. You may not be a doctor or a therapist, but just someone other people trust for advice. Mindfulness can help you become a better listener, which means you are going to be able to give much better advice than before you began practicing mindfulness. You will also find that when you are less judgmental about yourself, you will become less judgmental when it comes to other people. This is something people truly appreciate in someone they trust.

Another great benefit of mindfulness is that it helps to turn down the volume of your mind. **Did you know that we have thousands of thoughts every single day?** Our brains can go as far as having several thoughts within no more than a few seconds and while this is fascinating, it is quite annoying as well. If you are the type of person who pays attention to all of the thoughts that you have each day, you will find that it can seem as if a thousand people are talking in your head at the same time, and all of them are talking about completely different topics.

Mindfulness is going to allow you to shut all of these thoughts off. While it does take some work and time to get to that point, when you practice mindfulness meditation each day, you will have that 15 minutes or 30 minutes of time where there is nothing going on in your brain, and that is a very relaxing feeling.

I remember that at one point in my life, I found myself thinking that it would be wonderful if I was able to just not think at all. The reason for this was because my mind seemed to race at a million miles an hour. I would even wake up in the middle of the night with thoughts running through my head: figures, numbers, ideas and so on. I had so many thoughts that I had to write them down. I was tired and I was starting to burn out. I needed my mind to be quiet, even if it was only for a few minutes.

When you begin practicing mindfulness, you will find that it is quite difficult for you to do. However, when you continue to practice mindfulness, no matter where you are, you will be able to **completely shut your mind off simply by closing your eyes and taking a few breaths.** This means that when things are chaotic, out of control and you are not sure how you are supposed to react or if you find that your thoughts are screaming in your head demanding your attention, you will be able to take a few moments to yourself, practice mindfulness and completely clear your mind.

There are four main elements in mindfulness that help us in all areas of our life. They are: awareness of our body, regulation of emotion, self-awareness, and regulation of attention. These are the four main areas in a person's life that if they are gotten under control the person will quickly see a huge difference in their life.

These are the four areas that most problems in a person's life boil down to; some of us have more problem with one of them than others. Usually, we spend all our time and energy on improving any one or two of these aspects of our life, which leaves the rest of our life in a turmoil. When you are using mindfulness, you will find that you are not only focusing on one of these areas, but that you are focusing on all four which means that you are going to see huge amounts of improvement in your life.

One study showed that when a person practices mindfulness, they actually become better people. The study also showed that those who practice mindfulness, become more aware of who they truly are on the inside. When this happens, they are more likely to become the type of people that go around doing good and helping others. The reason for this is because mindfulness takes the focus of oneself, but it also forces the person practicing it to really understand how great their life is because they are becoming more aware of everything that they do. Every moment of their every day is spent in becoming more and more aware of all of the details of their life, realizing just how good it really is.

A very strange benefit of mindfulness is that when people practice mindfulness, they do not suffer from loneliness. We live in a world with billions of other people, but still many of us feel completely alone. Some people choose to spend their lives alone, others don't seem to have a choice; but the common factor is that everyone at some point or another, feels lonely. Loneliness affects some people much worse than it affects others; an introvert loves to be alone and often chooses to be alone over being around other people. But, there are people who simply cannot stand to be alone. They cannot deal with feeling lonely and they fill all of their time with other people. Nevertheless, at some point, all of us will feel lonely, even if we choose to spend our time alone. This is where mindfulness will make the difference in your life.

Mindfulness is going to show you that no, you are not alone. With mindfulness, you can finally feel that you are part of something huge. Even if you spend all of your time alone, instead of focusing on being alone, you are going to be able to focus on what you are doing. Whether you are dozing off in a chair, going for a walk or having a meal, you will be aware of every second of your life. You are also going to become more aware of everyone that you have in your life, those people that are always there for you and that while they may not be with you physically that moment, you still matter to them.

Mindfulness has many health benefits, as well. One of these is that, it boosts your immune system. **Studies have proven that those who practice mindfulness on a regular basis miss fewer days of work because of physical illnesses. When they do become sick, the symptoms are reduced and the person does not feel as sick as any other person would.**

If you are trying to lose weight or improve your fitness, mindfulness can make it easier to do. Becoming aware of what you are putting into your body is the first step to losing weight. I don't know how many times I have heard people say that they eat healthy, don't overeat and lead a very active life, but still gain weight. When I ask them if they have kept a food and activity journal, they tell me no. It is at this point that I know why they are having a hard time losing weight.

I stated earlier in this book, that people tend to only see the positive aspects about themselves. So, while a person may be munching on chips and chocolate most of the day while they lounge on the couch, what will stick out in their head is that orange that they ate and the 15 minutes of exercise that they got. However, when they become mindful of what they really are putting into their bodies and how much they are exercising, they realize that they have been fooling themselves.

When you practice mindfulness, you won't even need a food and fitness journal because you will automatically become aware of what you are putting into your body and how it makes your body feel. You will become aware of the amount of exercise you are getting and what is happening to your body because of the choices that you are making.

You see, we can go through our lives living in somewhat of a haze, not really conscious even though we and everyone that we are around thinks that we are. The state of non-consciousness is something that can last for years: the feeling of not really being present in your own life. Waking up from this is literally just like waking up. When you practice mindfulness, you will one day feel as if you opened your eyes, you may feel as if you suddenly reentered your body; you might feel as if you were having a dream and suddenly it ended.

Mindfulness will not only provide you with all of these benefits, but suddenly, you will feel as if you are living for the first time in your life. While that may seem strange to read right now, when it finally happens to you, you will completely understand what I am talking about.

Until then, welcome to the wonderful world of mindfulness.

Chapter 3- Mindfulness for Everyday Life

When you begin practicing mindfulness, it may seem a bit confusing and even a little overwhelming. But if you remember, I challenged you in the beginning of this book, to really pay attention to the words that you were reading. What I challenged you was to be mindful of the words that you were reading, to catch yourself when your mind began to wander and to bring your mind back to the task that you were doing: **reading this book.**

Now you may be sitting there thinking about the tasks that you do every day and telling yourself that there is no reason for you to be mindful of many of them. **After all, doing the dishes does not require much mindfulness, does it? You simply have to do them and get through them, but is that really the case?**

Have you ever actually felt the hot water on your hands as you manually washed your dishes? Have you breathed in the smell of the dish soap and felt the heaviness of the dishes in your hands? That is what it means to practice mindfulness in your everyday life. It means that no matter what task you are doing that you focus completely on that task and while it may be difficult when you find your mind wandering, you bring your mind back to the task at hand and do not think about anything else. You completely clear your mind of everything except what you are doing.

As I sit here writing this book, I can tell you that it could not be done without mindfulness. I am aware of the environment around me, of all of the noises that I hear and smells, but I am also very aware of the words that I am typing on this page. When my mind starts to drift, I have two choices, I can either allow it to drift and not complete this book, or I can bring it back to what I am doing and complete the task at hand.

Our minds are hard wired to think all of the time, and they are wired to drift from what we are doing, especially if the task seems boring to us or if it is not mentally stimulating. However, we have to remember that we are in control of our minds and not the other way around.

Mindfulness may sound complicated to you at this point, but the truth is, it is the farthest thing from complex. **It is simply the act of paying attention, using a certain technique, at the moment that you are living at the present, and doing this in a way that is completely nonjudgmental.** That really is all that there is to it. Of course, there are other things such as meditation that you can do in order to make the mindfulness easier, but while they do make the results appear faster, they are not necessary.

The <u>first thing</u> that I want you to do in order to bring mindfulness into your everyday life is to practice

mindfulness while you are taking part in your daily activities.

You need to become aware of how the water feels on your skin when you are taking a shower, become aware of how the toothbrush feels on your teeth and gums when you brush your teeth, or concentrate on the taste of the toothpaste. You have to become aware of what your food looks like, smells like, tastes like and how it feels in your mouth. You should become aware of what it feels like to walk or become aware of what it feels like to breath, how it feels when air fills your lungs and travels down your airways. When you do this, you will find that the things you do every day, the things that most of us take for granted are much more interesting than you thought they were.

The second thing that you should do in order to bring mindfulness into your everyday life is to start practicing as soon as you wake up in the morning.

So, the next morning after finishing this book, do not jump out of the bed as soon as the alarm clock goes off; do not start your morning thinking about all of the things that you need to get done that day but instead, take a few moments and practice mindfulness.

Begin by taking a nice stretch before you get up, as well as a few deep breaths. This is very important because what happens when you wake up is going to set the tone for your entire day. While most people know this, they do not do anything about it, but let the rest of the world set the tone. Instead, you are going to decide exactly how your day will go as soon as you wake up.

After you have taken a few deep breaths, become aware of the sun shining through your window, the birds chirping outside, maybe the sound of little feet creeping across the floor as your children begin their day, or the smell of coffee brewing in the pot. Look at your surroundings and remind yourself of the life that you really live. Be grateful for everything that you have in your life, not just material possessions, but the people that you love, your job, friends and so forth. Gratitude is going to go a long way when it comes to creating a happier and more successful life.

This does not have to take more than a few moments. However, if you are having a hard time being mindful, focus on your breathing and nothing else. Clear your mind for a few moments, feel the air as you inhale and exhale. Is it cold? What does it smell like? How does it make your body feel? That is all that it takes to start your day with mindfulness. If, however, you find that you doze off when you are doing this, practice while you are drinking your morning coffee, or step outside on your deck and practice. **It takes less than five minutes to change your entire day.**

Give your mind the freedom to wander a little. It is not possible for your mind to grasp the concept of mindfulness on your first try. I stated earlier in this book that your mind is naturally going to wonder and you should not feel as if you have to force it to stop all of the time. In order to make mindfulness work, you have to put time aside each day to let your mind wander. You see, the problem does not come when our mind wanders but when we focus on the thoughts that we are having. When you take time to allow your mind to wander, you will find that your mind is able to have thoughts but you don't have to engage in them. Gently let the thought pass until you can get your mind back to its mindful state.

Sit down for only 10 to 15 minutes a day, and simply allow your mind to wander. As random thoughts come into your mind, acknowledge your unwanted thoughts instead of trying to push them aside, but do not focus on it. Let the thoughts disappear just as fast as they appeared and allow your mind to move on to the next. Soon you are going to learn that while your mind can easily wander, you are not required to focus on them. This will enable you to be able to practice mindfulness in your life while not being distracted by the hundreds of thoughts that crowd your mind.

When you find yourself getting distracted throughout the day, try and bring your thoughts back to what you are doing, but understand in the beginning this may only last for a few moments. As you practice mindfulness more and more, you will not have to remind yourself as much. Rather, you will find that you are mindful more often than you are not. There are still going to be times that your mind wanders, but they are nothing to worry about. Simply take a deep breath, center yourself, clear your mind and go back to the task that you want to focus on.

Keep things short. In the beginning of your journey of mindfulness, when you are focusing on one task, do not expect your mind to stay focused for long. A total of 20 minutes of practice should be enough the first few times. Actually, this is the maximum time you should spend in a day trying to learn mindfulness. Practicing mindfulness when you are at home, taking part in short activities is almost like lifting weights for the brain. It works the brain just like lifting weights does a muscle and ensures that it is able to endure longer sessions down the road. Later, when you have grown more accustomed to mindfulness, you can practice for longer.

One great thing about mindfulness is that it can be practiced everywhere, so while you may not have 30 minutes per day to really focus on mindfulness meditation, chances are you are spending at least that amount of time waiting every single day. Practice mindfulness while you are on hold, while you wait in line, or while you are waiting for your meal to be brought to your table. There are so many times in our lives that we are waiting for something to happen and those moments are simply taken from us. But if you fill that time with mindfulness, you are not only taking advantage of every moment that you have in your life but you are also reaping the benefits of mindfulness at the same time.

You don't have to focus on everything that is going on around you; this is another time when you can simply focus on your breathing and clear your mind. **But be careful! Do not close your eyes unless it is safe for you to do so.** For example, do not close your eyes to be mindfulness when you are driving, taking care of a baby, operating machinery or cooking.

Pick a trigger. Did that make sense? Let me explain.

Most habits are formed because there is a trigger that makes you perform the habit. For example, a smoker picks up a cigarette when they feel stressed; this is because it is likely stress is the main reason why they began to smoke. They may have started smoking when they were stressed about an exam in college, or stressed before a big presentation at work. If that's how they started smoking, that particular person will think of smoking every time they are stressed, for whatever reason, even after they have quit.

When you are cleaning your house, you probably go on autopilot because you have made a habit out of how you clean. You may work through each room in a specific order and each activity in each room in a specific order. You need to create the same type of trigger for being mindful.

Suppose your trigger is to drink a cup of coffee every time you sit down on your deck, desk or balcony. Combine this trigger with mindfulness so that for the next two months or more, every time you sit down on your deck/desk/balcony, with or without a cup of coffee, you remember to be mindful. It could just be a 10-minute break that you take in the middle of a busy day, but it will become your daily reminder to practice mindfulness.

While mindfulness is about getting out of autopilot, creating this trigger will ensure that you are taking part in mindfulness, which will make you more aware of what you are doing throughout the rest of your day.

One of the most important things that you will need to do to practice mindfulness is to learn how to meditate. Meditation is simply the best way for you to encourage mindfulness in your day-to-day life. **We will cover mindfulness meditation in a later chapter,** but I encourage you to take part in other forms of meditation as well. For example, if you are having a hard time with productivity, practice meditation for productivity; if you are having a hard time staying positive in life, practice positive meditation, and so forth. I can guarantee it will change your life for the better.

While mindfulness meditation can be learned if you have never meditated before, it is best to brush up a bit on meditation and learn how to do it before you take part in it. Let us imagine that meditation is language as a whole, where mindfulness meditation is a specific language; let's say, English. A person who have never spoken or learned English before can't suddenly start speaking it, just because they decide to try it. They would have to learn the language, practice it regularly, and then hope to be an expert in it. Although learning meditation or mindfulness is neither so time-consuming nor as hard as learning a language, you'll still need time.

There are however great guided meditations that you can find online for free that will help you through the process. Learning mindfulness meditation is not complicated, but it does take some getting used to. On the positive side, when you practice any type of meditation, you will see huge changes taking place in your life, right from the way that you look at the events that are happening in your life and experience them to how you feel about yourself as a person and the people that you attract into your life.

Using mindfulness in your day to day life is not only going to help you use it when things get rough, but it is going to start to rewire your brain. Imagine how great you will feel when you know that simply by using mindfulness while you brush your hair or your teeth, you are forever changing your life. **It is a great feeling to really live every moment in your life instead of being somewhere else mentally, someplace other than where your body physically is.** There is also a great peace that comes with practicing mindfulness that you can understand only when you've experienced it firsthand.

Chapter 4- Using Mindfulness to Change Your Life

Before you start practicing mindfulness, you need to understand exactly how it can change your life. The answer is simple: while mindfulness has many benefits and it affects a person's life in many ways, it will change your life because when you are using mindfulness, you are focusing on the smallest of details within your life. Instead of letting your life pass by you, you are going to focus on the experience that you are having right then and there, whether it be good or bad one. You are not attaching yourself to the experience nor are you struggling against the experience; you are simply living the experience.

Being mindful means finally accepting that certain things are going to happen in your life that are going to be completely out of your control. It also means that while something negative may be happening right in front of your eyes, you know you are bigger than that one tiny event and that you would not let it bring you down. In fact, you would understand that it might just be something that pushes you to a better future, but you don't really worry about what that future is going to be because you are living in your present.

How many times has someone told you not to take today for granted because there may not be a tomorrow? Well, of course, there will be a tomorrow for some people, but not for everyone. However, that shouldn't stop us from living today, should it? Mindfulness ensures that instead of you focusing on the past - which has already happened and cannot be changed, or on the future - which is not promised to any of us, we focus on right now.

Before we move on, I want to make something perfectly clear.

Mindfulness does not mean that we do not have to pay our bills or go to work because we are living in this moment right now and not worrying about tomorrow.

We still have to be adults and do all of the boring things adults do; we still have to look for a job, pay our bills, make dinner, and save money for the future. But at the same time, we can use mindfulness to reduce your stress when it comes to figuring out how those bills are going to be paid. **Mindfulness is about enhancing your life, not taking the easy way out.** It does not mean that we do not have to learn from our mistakes or that we should float through life; it simply means that we actually live every minute of our lives instead of always worrying about the next, or thinking about the moments long gone from our lives.

Mindfulness is going to change your life because instead of being a victim of our emotions, we can begin to understand why we feel the way that we do. With mindfulness, the way we are feeling will end just as quickly as it began, and there will be no reason to let our emotion control how we react to

something.

If you really sit back and think about it, I bet you will recognize what I am about to explain next; bet it has happened to your own life many times. Someone, possibly you, gets upset over something that has happened in their life and from that moment on, even for weeks, they focus on that single tiny event and let the emotions they are feeling dictate how they will live.

Now this is not to say that you can never be upset, feel sad or angry; of course, you'll experience different emotions but after practicing mindfulness, you will be able to truly feel your emotions. You can't force yourself not to feel any emotions or hold on to your feeling for weeks; but you will be able to feel them and move on from them.

At the same time, it is also important that you learn how to control your emotions. **When I say that you should feel your emotions, I do not mean that you should break down crying and collapse on the floor because something did not go your way. Rather, you should learn to react to them appropriately and move forward with your life.** When you do this, you will find that you have finally acquired **inner peace.** You won't always have to hold back your emotions if you learn to react to them **appropriately.**

If you know that your emotions are out of control and that you are overreacting to minor events, it is important that you make the decision to start maturing emotionally right now. While I cannot go into all of the aspects of emotional maturity in this book, I can tell you this, there are plenty of books and online resources that can help you mature emotionally.

While everything in the world is changing and everyone around you are racing to keep up, anyone who practices mindfulness is going to have <u>inner peace.</u> They are going to be able to find stillness in a world where it is a rarity. You will find that you can finally let go of all of the judgments that you have held on to in the past, not just about yourself but about the people around you.

Of course, you are still going to have to be selective about the people you let into your life. After all, we have to face the reality! There will always be some people that we simply do not want in our lives, but you can finally learn not to feel judgmental towards them.

While everything in the world is changing and people are racing to keep up, a person who practices mindfulness is going to have inner peace. They are going to be able to find stillness in a world where stillness is a rarity.

You will find that you let go of all of the judgments that you have held on to in the past, not just about yourself but about the people around you.

Let's face it, no matter who we are, we have all judged other people at one point or another in our lives, even people we have just met. This is one of the reasons that many people become insecure about themselves, because they feel other people judging them as they have judged others. Mindfulness allows you to stop being judgmental when it comes to yourself and understand why things happen; it also teaches you to be more sympathetic to the people that you encounter on a day-to-day basis.

This happens for two reasons. Firstly, because you are so aware of your own feelings and what is going on in your own life, you simply do not have the time to focus on the faults of others. Secondly, you become a completely self-aware person who, all of a sudden, realize that you're not quite as perfect as you thought you were. Suddenly, you begin to understand that you were so judgmental toward others in the past because you saw the faults in them that bother you in yourself.

When you experience mindfulness, you will suddenly realize that you have been walking around in a fog your entire life. Yes, you had been awake, but finally you would be awakened. When the fog finally lifts, you'll not only be able to see your life, but the entire world as it really is. It will be as if you are being reborn into an entirely new world.

There's one more thing that I want to clear right now: **while mindfulness is great, it is not a magic pill that is going to take away all of the stress you have to deal with each day.** Your kids are still going to misbehave, you are still going to have to go to work, you are still going to have to clean your house and you are still going to have to mow the lawn. However, **mindfulness is going**

to make all of that so much easier for you to deal with.

When you start to practice mindfulness, here's one of the things that you will begin to understand: you are not the combination of your thoughts; you are not your job, you are not your titles or the amount of your paycheck. These are simply factors that describe the different roles that you play in your life. Your thoughts are simply that, **thoughts.** For example, when someone talks about healing, they talk about mind, body and spirit. We all have a body, we have to live in it every day. Most of us understand that somewhere within that body, is a spirit, and then we get to the mind.

Right now, I want you to ask yourself where your mind is. Is it the brain? Do you think that your mind is in your brain, where your thoughts come from? What happens when you change your mind? Is your brain somehow changing, too? No. Your brain is a part of the body; your brain is only a third of the person you are; it is a part of what makes you up. This is important to understand, because I have seen a lot of people get angry at themselves for a though that has crossed their mind. **They allow the thoughts that pass through their mind to define who they are**.

For example, one smart-alecky thought can make someone feel as if that is who they are, when in reality they are quite sweet. If you allow these thoughts to define you, then you are not living as your true self.

This is a reason why we should think about what we want to say before it comes out of our mouths. We know that our minds can spout off a bit but that does not mean that we have to. The truth is that, we all as humans have to put our thoughts in check now and then. If you were a surmise of your thoughts, you wouldn't be the person you are.

We all have negative thoughts at some point or another, but we don't have to believe all of them. All parents have extremely bad days when they decide it was a mistake to have children, but no one believes it wholeheartedly. We all have good days and bad days, but not all the thoughts that crosses our mind are important.

You can do one of two things: you can allow your thoughts to define who you are and be that terrible parent; or, you can realize that no you are not a terrible parent that you are doing the best that you can, and that is all that anyone can ask from you.

Even as adults, we find ourselves reacting badly to the things that are happening around us. Usually it is done without a lot of class or in a way that can be damaging for us, and for those that we love the most. If a mother negatively reacts every time their child throws a fit, it will damage her relationship with her entire family. Although the wrong approach, reacting negatively to your child's tantrums doesn't make anyone a bad parent. This is just a habit that can be rectified, and it doesn't define who you are. **When you practice mindfulness, you will quickly be triggered to take a breath, clear your mind and react to the situation in a way that will be productive.**

Do you know what that means? **No more screaming fits with the two-year-old!**

When you practice mindfulness, you also become

more grateful. Even though you have fixed your daughter's hair a million times, you will find these little things to be grateful for. You will start enjoying chores like fixing her hair because you have never experienced fixing her hair at this moment, at this exact time, with her being exactly who she is right now ever before.

But how is all of this supposed to happen? It is important for you to understand one of the basic fundamentals of life. You are right now what you think about most in your life. If you are struggling to make ends meet, it is not because you are not working hard, it is because that is what you are focusing on all of the time. Think about it like this: have you ever noticed that when good things happen to you, more good things follow? For example, have you noticed that when you are not worried about your money, you have more money coming in, or more chances to make money?

What about the old saying "when it rains, it pours"? I am sure we have all experienced this. When something negative happens in our lives, it seems like everything comes crumbling down all at once. It's the same with positive events.

Have you ever stopped to really think about why that is? If you have ever taken the time to learn about "The Secret", then you know that it is because **a person is what they think about the most**. If you have never taken the time to understand this, I suggest that you do more research. The basic idea is this: if you are always focused on the bills that you have to pay and the lack of funds to pay them with, that is what you are going to get out of life. On the other hand, if you are focused on all of the great things that you are going to buy with your extra money, that is what you are going to bring into your life.

This also means that if you are always telling yourself you are a bad parent, that is exactly what you are going to be! The only way to change that is to begin telling yourself that you are a good parent. Let it out! Speak out! **The tongue is more powerful than people give it credit for. When we use our words, we can literally change the way that we feel about ourselves.**

When you practice mindfulness, you are going to become more aware of these positive thoughts. So the next time a negative thought enters your head, you will quickly become aware of it and you will change the thought to a more positive one. For every "I'll never be able to do this", there should be a "I know that I can get this done quickly."

This may sound like a bit of hooey, but give it a chance and I guarantee that by becoming more aware of your thoughts and changing them that you will see dramatic changes in your life.

You'll also discover that you have created a story about yourself. This story is usually created on the basis of your past experiences and you are going to do whatever you need to do in order to reinforce this story in your own mind. If you are divorced, you may feel that you are damaged and no one will ever want you. Some people go as far as gaining a tremendous amount of weight simply so that they can push other people away, ensuring that they are unable to have a successful relationship. Others isolate themselves from those of the opposite sex and still, others seek out specific people that they know are not ready for a successful relationship. All of this reinforces their opinion of themselves.

However, when you become mindful, you will begin to understand that the story you have been telling yourself may not be as true as you once thought it was.

The great thing is that you can rewrite that story, reinforce who you really want to be and before you know it, you will be that person.

Chapter 5-Mindfulness for Productivity

Productivity is something a lot of people are struggling with today, simply because we have so many distractions. We have our phones, email, social media, televisions, our families and then there are, of course, the **mental distractions.**

Most books on productivity will tell you that you need to eliminate the distractions in order for you to become more productive. That is fine when it comes to the **external distractions** but what can you do about the **internal distractions**?

The main reason why people struggle with productivity is because of the internal distractions, not the external. Of course, while the external distractions can take your focus away from what you are doing for a moment, it is the internal distractions that seem to take up the most amount of time.

Have your thoughts pulled you away from this book while you were reading it? Did you wonder what you would have for dinner, if you had paid the electric bill, if you would make enough money next week to purchase that new pair of shoes? Maybe you found yourself thinking about the events of the past or wondering about the future.

Maybe you have begun to notice that this happens to you quite a bit as you go about your day-to-day life. Perhaps you find that while you are sitting at your desk at work, you are somewhere else mentally. These are the distractions that are not so easy to shut off.

I have done a lot of studying over the last several years about productivity and I have learned one thing that I wish I knew earlier in my life. I wish I knew how to shut off my internal distractions. This would have removed a huge amount of stress from my life and would have allowed me to become much more productive that I was.

When we practice mindfulness, we become much more aware of what we are doing and what we are supposed to be doing. This means that instead of taking a break every five minutes to check our social media accounts, we can quickly recognize the moment that we are distracted and bring ourselves back to what we were doing in the first place.

Mindfulness increases our focus. While right now it may seem impossible for you to stay on task because you are unable to focus for a long period of time, when you use mindfulness, you will find that your work is completed quickly and that you were able to focus the entire time.

Think about it like this. You are working on a big project when all of a sudden you feel the need to check your email because who knows, the elite might be taking over the world at this very moment and if you don't check, you will never know! While you are checking your email, you see that you received one from Amazon, stating that you still had items in your cart. Suddenly you remember why you left them in your cart. There was another item that you wanted to look for, so you jump on over to Amazon and start searching. You suddenly remember that you've been meaning to buy a new skirt for a date the next week, and you start browsing for clothes. You can't really stop after choosing a skirt, not when there's a sale on shoes....

Before you know it, you've spend a whole hour on your phone and it is already lunch time. You look at the progress you have made on your project and realize, you are going to have to take it home and work on it... yet again!

When you practice mindfulness, none of this is going to happen because as soon as you **begin thinking about your email, you are going to become aware of it, you are going to take a deep breath** and realize that no one is taking over the planet, that there is nothing in that email that cannot wait until the project is done and at this very moment in your life you are supposed to be working on the project! How's that for increased productivity?

The moment that you think about something else other than work, you will become aware of your environment. You will remember that you are at work and the task you are trying to allow yourself to be distracted by is not something that should be done at work. You are going to remind yourself that you have never before in your life worked on this specific project and **that it is something you will enjoy doing.** You won't enjoy anything else that you will enjoy working at that moment, and not stop until you've finished working.

All of this is going to happen in a matter of seconds and you will quickly be back on task. When lunch time arrives, you are going to be done with the project and ready to move on to the next. After a much-deserved break, you will smile to yourself because on that night, you do not have to take your work home with you.

Another way that mindfulness is going to allow you to be more productive is that it is going to help you to plan better. While it may seem that planning and mindfulness do not go together since when you practice mindfulness, you do not worry about the future, that is in fact not the reality.

Most of the stress that we face in our lives is because we are worried about a negative outcome in the future. We are not facing stress because we are daydreaming about the wonderful future that we want unless that is causing us to become unproductive people. While it would be perfectly stress-free if we only focused on this second right now, the truth is that we would not really get a lot done.

Since our minds are able to think about the future and worry about the future, we need to be able to take advantage of this. Moreover, we can do this by planning. When you practice mindfulness, you learn how to change those negative thoughts about the future into thoughts about the present. You can also use this technique to ensure that there really is nothing to worry about.

Let's imagine that you have so much to do tomorrow that you are not sure that you can get it all done. If you sit down and create a schedule for the day, ensuring that you fit everything in with an ample amount of time to complete it, you will be able to reduce your stress. You need to keep the schedule with you the next day; whenever you feel that you are starting to get distracted from what you need to be doing, glance at the schedule and it is going to trigger mindfulness.

This means that you are going to be able to stay on task and complete all of your tasks without getting distracted, simply because you were mindful of what you were doing.

Everyone knows that sleep is one of the most important factors in our life when it comes to productivity, and yet we tend to not get enough of it. This is mainly because we don't always go to bed in time to get eight hours of sleep, and because we are usually lying in bed worrying about the sales figures, or lie in bed playing games on our phone.

We definitely need enough sleep at night if we want to be productive during the day. When you are in bed, you need to put the phone down, turn off the television in your bedroom, and get rid of any kind of external distractions. You need to be absolutely comfortable in your bed, and bring your focus back into your body. You need to become aware of how tired your body is, how comfortable the bed is, how warm the blanket feels around your body and how soft the pillow is under your head. You need to feel the cool air from the fan touching your face, and hear the deep breaths that you are taking. Before you know it, you'll fall asleep and have a good night's sleep.

If you can fall asleep in your bed using mindfulness technique, you are going to wake the next morning refreshed, focused and ready to start your day. You see, mindfulness does not have to be used only when we are at work or when we are completing some task, but it can be used to help us do the simple things that we need to do, such as, falling asleep.

The great thing about mindfulness is that it can be practiced wherever you are. While many companies have begun to understand how mindfulness affects productivity and have begun using it in the workplace, there are still those that have not. However, when you practice mindfulness meditation - which we will talk more about in the next chapter, you don't have to worry about chanting, or sit cross-legged, or even close your eyes while you are at work.

Wherever you are, all that you have to do to practice mindfulness is to take a few deep breathes and become mindful of the way that you are feeling, your thoughts and your breaths.

When you do this, you are literally training your brain so that the next time you become distracted, it is easier for you to bring your focus back to the task at hand. If you continue to practice this, you will find out that you really don't have to remind yourself to be mindful and productive any longer; it will start to come naturally to you after a while.

In order to do this, make sure that you start to practice mindfulness as soon as you arrive at work. You can set a timer for every 2 hours or whatever time is convenient for you, and spend a few minutes practicing. Every time you hear the timer, it will remind you that you are supposed to be practicing mindfulness. Continue doing this for about a week until you find that you no longer need the 2-hour timer; your mind will automatically know when it's time to start practicing. You can even double the amount of time on the timer, making it four or five hours before you have to practice again.

When this becomes natural to you and you are able to practice mindfulness without the timer, double it again and again until you no longer need the reminder to be mindful at work. But don't let mindfulness stop there; when you arrive home, practice mindfulness again.

The changes that you will see in your life are tremendous. Hopefully, by this point in this book, you are able to understand just how amazing this technique is and <u>how it can change your life.</u>

Chapter 6-Mindfulness Meditation

As you have hopefully learned throughout this book, mindfulness is a truly great way to reduce stress in your life, improve your health, as well as the quality of your life. **It is the best way for you to make the changes in your life that you want to see; if you want to change your life into one you want to enjoy, you need to start practicing mindfulness right now.**

In this chapter, I want to cover **mindfulness meditation.** I have talked a bit about mediation earlier in this book, but there is actually a specific kind of meditation that will help to improve your mindfulness, which means that you will begin to see some benefits much faster.

Steps to do Mindfulness Meditation

1. **The first thing** that you want to do when you are preparing for any mediation is to choose a place. This should be a location that is comfortable for you, one where you will be free from distraction and will not be interrupted.

   Many people like to prepare the environment by lighting a few candles, playing some relaxing music, using bells, burning incense or even opening a window to allow them to breathe in the fresh air. When you are preparing your environment, it is best for you to place meaningful items in the environment. You may choose to place a picture that makes you feel calm and relaxed, or an object that makes you feel close to a loved one.

It is important that your meditation environment is free from clutter, that it is clean and does not contain any object which would cause you stress. **While you do not have to devote an entire room to your meditation, it is best if you can have at least a small corner dedicated to your meditation practices.** This will ensure that mediating does not become a chore, and you won't have to gather all of the items every time that you want to meditate. Besides, you will be reminded to meditate every time you pass this particular area in your home.

2. **The next thing** that you will want to do is to change into comfortable clothing. You do not want to be wearing anything that is too restrictive or that will take your focus off of the meditation. In other words, loose comfortable clothing that does not restrict your breathing is great for meditating in.

   Once you have changed your clothing, you can sit in whatever position is most comfortable for you. Some people prefer to sit in a cross-legged position while others are more comfortable lying down in their meditation space. It is important to note that you may fall asleep while you are meditating and if this happens, it could mean that you are not getting enough sleep at night, or that you are more tired than you should be. While it is usually okay for you to fall asleep during meditation, especially guided meditation, mindfulness meditation is more interactive and requires you to stay awake. Unless you are lying in bed and using mindfulness meditation to help you fall asleep - as we discussed previously, you need to stay focused during mindful meditation.

WHILE YOU DO NOT HAVE TO DEVOTE AN ENTIRE ROOM, IT IS BEST IF YOU CAN HAVE AT LEAST A SMALL CORNER WHICH IS DEDICATED TO YOUR MEDITATION PRACTICES.

THIS WILL ENSURE THAT MEDIATING DOES NOT BECOME A CHORE, YOU WILL NOT HAVE TO GATHER ALL OF THE ITEMS EVERY TIME THAT YOU WANT TO MEDITATE AND YOU WILL BE REMINDED TO MEDITATE EVERY TIME YOU PASS THE AREA IN YOUR HOME.

Sometimes, you might feel the need to move or add a pillow, or sit on a rolled-up towel to be comfortable, and that is completely fine. Allow yourself several minutes to find the position that works best for you. You may find that a position that worked well for you yesterday does not work well for you today, simply because you took part in different activities and different parts of your body are sore. Whichever position is comfortable for you works in meditation; you can even lie down if you want to, but just don't fall asleep.

You will also want to make sure that you set time aside. When you are just starting out, you may not be able to practice for more than a few minutes and that is okay, but it seems that 20 minutes is the magic number. Studies have found that when a person meditates for 20 minutes each day using mindfulness meditation, they benefit much more than those who would meditate for 15 or even 30 minutes.

If you have decided on meditating for 20 minutes, you need to make sure that nothing interferes with it. Of course, life happens and there are going to be times that you are not going to be able to meditate, but do not make a habit out of this. Mindfulness meditation is not going to work if you only practice it when you remember or have extra time. This has to be a regular part of your life.

3. **You should begin meditating by taking a few deep breaths.** Inhale through your nose and out your mouth, releasing all of the stress of the day. **Focus only on your breathing**, and nothing else. Don't think about missed deadline, or arguments with your partner, or on the bills that need to be paid. **Let all of the events that have happened that day flow from your mind and focus on the feel of the air around you, the sounds and smells in your environment, and your own breaths.**

You do not have to change the way that you breathe while you are doing this. Many people think that they have to take these long, deep unnatural breaths, but I assure you, your body knows how to breathe without you interfering.

At some point, your mind is going to begin to wander

and you are going to have random thoughts enter your mind. This is okay. Having thoughts is one of the great things about being human. When this happens, remind yourself that you are not your thoughts and that you have control over the thoughts that you think. Bring your focus back to your breathing.

If you begin to feel emotions welling to the surface that you do not want to engage in, simply acknowledge them and release them, bringing your thoughts back to your breathing. Do not be surprised if you end up crying during the first few meditations, especially if you are dealing with a lot of stress. When you meditate, you will be releasing these emotions. This can happen especially if you have had a particularly hard time lately, because this is the only time you are relaxed enough to allow it to do so.

If you want to cry, cry. However, do not allow yourself to focus on the event that caused the negative emotions in you. Remind yourself that it is in the past and that you are focusing on the present. Bring your focus back to your breathing. Do not beat yourself up about the thoughts that enter your mind. This practice is all about no judgment so if a negative thought enters your mind, acknowledge it and let it go. Don't focus on it and don't judge yourself because of it. There is no reason for you to feel poorly about yourself because you had a thought that you don't think you should be having. As long as you do not focus on the thought, but on your breathing, you are going to be fine and your meditation is going to go great.

4. **Any time that you find yourself getting distracted** by the noises around you or things that have happened in your life, simply bring your focus back to your breathing. You see, our minds are not able to focus on more than one thing at a time. While many people think that they can focus on multiple topics at the same time, it is simply not possible. So, if you find that you are thinking about something else, you need to bring your focus to your breathing, and that random thought will slowly vanish from your mind.

When a thought enters our mind, we have two choices: we can focus on it and give it power; or, we can push the thought out of our mind and not allow it to have any control over us. This is what you want to do when any negative thought comes into your mind, at all points of your life.

You may feel a little strange at first when it comes to meditating, especially if you have never done it before. This is why I suggest that you meditate in an area that is away from your family members. You need to find a location where you won't be interrupted, watched or bothered. **It is quite difficult for some people to meditate when they feel as if they are being watched**.

Meditation is not a performance that should have an audience. If you are meditating simply to make people think a certain way about you, or to get the attention of those around you, then you have certainly chosen meditation for all the wrong reasons.

If you want to benefit from meditation, you

need to do it for the right reasons. Meditation should only be chosen when you want to see major changes in your life, not because you are trying to impress anyone.

5. While you are meditating, it is important that you focus on what is happening in your present. It is amazing the things you will remember when you are trying to meditate. You may remember an event that happened in high school that you thought did not affect you at all, but when the thought of it pops into your head, you suddenly realize it affected you more than you previously admitted. This is quite normal, perfectly fine and common. Your mind works in a completely different way when you are not overworking it, and it can pull up memories that you have consciously forgotten about.

Do not react. Instead, bring your focus back to what is happening right now, back to the meditation and let the thought pass without focusing on it. If you do find that you have been focusing on a thought and it will happen, simply acknowledge that you were not being mindful and bring yourself back to the meditation.

While this specific mediation is going to focus on you taking the time out of your day to separate yourself from the rest of your life, you do not have to do this if you don't have the time. **Mindfulness meditation can also be done while you are taking part in your regular activities.**

Here is an approach that is less formal, but still a technique that you can use when you're out and about. This is good to practice all through life, and it'll allow you to be in the present and allow you to stay fully aware. With this, you can choose a task and work on informal mindfulness, similar to what was said before, but you can use this with literally any other technique.

There are a few things to keep in mind when you're doing this, so make sure you follow adequately.

-Pay attention to the sensations in your body.

-Breathe in through your nose, let the air flow into your belly and expand, and then breathe out through your mouth. You should notice the complete inhale and exhale process.

-Continue to do whatever task it is slowly and with deliberation

-Start to engage your senses completely, with noticing each sight, various touches, and even sounds so that you can savor this. If you start to notice your mind wandering, bring it back to the sensations in the moment.

With mindfulness meditation, as you've seen here, there isn't much to it. But it's a technique that, though not very complicated, can still have extremely powerful results in your life.

Chapter 7: Myths About Mindfulness Meditation

You might wonder if there are any myths about mindfulness that you know about or have heard of. With mindfulness, the essence is to pay attention, and that is something that, in a society such as ours, is considered almost a foreign concept. It's a concept that has been around in Buddhism for thousands of years, and with it being pushed into mainstream culture, one might think there are special secret health benefits and myths that are true.

However, there are some myths that deserve to be debunked, and this chapter is going to go over a few of the important ones you should know.

1) Mindfulness and meditation are the same

That's not the case. While mindfulness can be practiced through meditation and through the events of our lives, they can be different. You can use mindfulness meditation by sitting down, walking about and noticing various parts of yourself, yoga, and even lying down. However, you can also use mindfulness to notice what is happening throughout the day, which is what many do. It's also important to know that with meditation, there are branches of it that are different. Even mindfulness meditation is different from mindfulness, so make sure that you know the difference before you are trying any or both of them.

2) Is Mindfulness all deep breathing ONLY?

It's not always that. When you're starting, it's important to make sure that you are breathing well and not super ragged, but you shouldn't always be focusing on taking deep breaths. In essence, if you want to take easier breaths, you can. There is no exact technique. We don't even need to count, take super deep breaths, or even change the mantra that we have.

In truth, it's really just using something as a catalyst to focus our attention. We need to put our attention on whatever we feel is the best for us, and then just go with the flow. That's what the intention of this is, not on breathing deep or breathing hard. When you are meditating, it's encouraged to take deep breaths, but it is all up to you, and you should work on whatever you believe is the best thing to believe.

3) The ultimate goal is to be in a blissful state

Another common misconception of this is to think your end goal is to be in some sort of nirvana state where you are just in pure, utter bliss. In mindfulness meditation, there is no objective to have a higher state of being, or even to reach nirvana. Even relaxation isn't supposed to be the end goal to this. Mindfulness meditation is used to help one look at whatever is happening within them with an open mind, acknowledging that those thoughts are there, that the bad experiences are coming about, that you're stressed out, and working got not let these feelings affect you as well.

It's not a guarantee that mindfulness is going to work for every one of us. Sometimes too much awareness can freak us out, and we might hit up old wounds. But you can also use mindfulness to see these things, mustering the courage as they are rather than in some pipe dream.

You might have inner conflicts that still need to be healed by a good counselor, but that doesn't mean that you can't get away from the thoughts by acknowledging that are there. With mindfulness and mindful meditation, you're looking at the direct problems, seeing them for what they are, and over time, you acknowledge them. Soon, you start to notice what it is that will bring these thoughts up, in order to help you engage in a positive change that is working for you.

Mindfulness isn't just trying to reach nirvana; it's about handling the unpleasant situations so that you're not at the receiving end of these bad effects anymore.

4) The Sole Goal is to be Present in the moment of all time

It isn't. The goal of mindfulness might seem to be present fully in the moment 24/7, but let's look at it this way. If we did that, we might just go crazy. While we do need to be distracted at times, we should also take the time to think out of the box as well. We should work with this not to smother the creative mindset that we have, but instead taking out the distractions that aren't good for us, and especially the emotions that are holding us back. You should never work to dampen your creative ability, but it would be best if you worked to make sure that you aren't letting bad thoughts take you away from your present moment.

5) You should always go for a quiet mind

You might think that the end-all goal of meditation is to be quiet mentally, but that's not the case. Many are actually doing it wrong if they only think that. It is more of a mental control than anything. If you think it's all about blocking out feelings and thoughts, then you're going to have another thing coming. With mindfulness, you shouldn't work to block your thoughts, but what you should do instead is to start looking through them as they go along, acknowledging that they are there, and then going back to the task at hand, which is on our breathing.

We're always going to think thoughts, worries, planning, solving, and looking at old memories from the past. However, you don't have to block out everything so that your mind is quiet; but rather, what you're doing is looking for the thoughts that are sucking up our energy, are creating worries within, and in general just put us in a bad mood.

It's about making sure that the bad thoughts don't plague your mind, but rather, they're there, acknowledged, and not made much more than that.

Conclusion

Mindfulness meditation is a great way for you to turn your life around, to make it the life that you want it to be and to take action ensuring that you can experience more happiness than ever before.

If you have found that no matter what you try, you just can't seem to get things together in your life, mindfulness meditation may be the answer and I encourage you to give it a try.

With that being said though, it's time to go over the next step. Your next step is simple, and that is to start on your journey to mindfulness in ways that are correct for you. Look at yourself, see where you need to improve. Practice mindfulness meditation, and from there, you'll be able to harness the power of yourself, seeing what distractions lay bare for you, and working to overcome them.

I hope that you found this book interesting as well as educational. I hope that it has helped you to understand mindfulness, how you can put it to work for you in your life and how you can benefit from it.